HOLD ON TO YOUR FORKS!

THE BEST IS YET TO COME

BONNIE BRUCE

Creative Force Press

Creative Force Press

Hold on to Your Forks!
© 2014 by Bonnie Bruce

This title is also available as an eBook. Visit www.CreativeForcePress.com/titles for more information.

Published by Creative Force Press
4704 Pacific Ave, Suite C, Lacey, WA 98503
www.CreativeForcePress.com

All Scripture quotations, unless otherwise noted, are taken from the Holy Bible, ESV Study Bible, copyright 2008 by Crossway, a publishing ministry of Good News Publishers. All Rights reserved. ESV Text Edition, 2011.

All rights reserved. No part of this publication may be reproduced, stored in a retrieval system, or transmitted in any form or by any means--for example, electronic, photocopy, recording--without the prior written permission of the publisher, except for brief quotations in printed reviews. Views expressed in this work are solely those of the author. Author notes that some references are from remembered ideas, past read biblical passages, and multiple articles imbedded in her mind.

ISBN: 978-1-939989-14-7

Printed in the USA - For worldwide distribution

Dedication

Two amazing women have helped and supported me more than any other earthly people.

Ms. Joni Bailey was my very first sister in Christ. She has seen me in times of failure and achievements. She has walked with me during my highs and lows. She has loved and accepted me through every step of the way. I am forever grateful that God placed her in my path.

Mrs. Barbara Armstrong is the most joyful, loving person I have ever known. Her joy comes from her deep, ever growing love for Jesus Christ. She has single-handedly introduced me to the pure side of life. I cannot imagine ever finishing this "little" book without her on-going support and love.

1 Samuel 18:1 says, *"...the soul of Jonathan was knit to the soul of David."*

I am truly "knit-in-spirit" to these two wonderful women.

Table of Contents

Chapters:

1:	Yesterday's Child	7
2:	A Childhood Should Never Hurt	9
3:	"Uppity Women"	12
4:	"Mr. Right"	14
5:	A One-Parent View	17
6:	Tobacco Road	20
7:	All-American Family	22
8:	The Affairs	25
9:	Words Spoken	27
10:	A Mother's Failure	29
11:	Hello Love	32
12:	Freefall	35
13:	From the Ashes	37
14:	Introducing the Saints	39
15:	Journey Forward	41
16:	Me on Me	43
17:	The "Great Shepherd"	45
18:	Who Do You Say You Are?	48
19:	Let's Talk About Love	51
20:	Say a Little Prayer for You	54
21:	Faith vs. Fear	58
22:	Tell Me Why Again	61
23:	Pardon Me	63
24:	The Evolution of Me	66
25:	Life's Desserts	69

Questions and Suggestions	72
Epilogue	81
About the Author	83

Chapter 1

Yesterday's Child

She was born two months premature with a birth weight of only 3 pounds, 4 ounces, to an alcoholic mother, having what is now known as "fetal alcohol syndrome." These facts barely scratch the surface of this child's remarkable survival.

This child, you see, is me. The story actually begins a few weeks prior to my birth. I am the product of two failed abortion attempts. The simple fact that I survived is extraordinary by itself, but to do so without either a mental or physical deficit is nothing short of miraculous!

How do I know this fact about myself? My mother told me, repeatedly. She frequently voiced the synopsis to me throughout my childhood. I was the *mistake*, the *ugly child*, the *unwanted girl child*. My mother was an alcoholic. She was not the occasional social drinker, nor was she the jolly, comical drinker. She was the abusive, brutal, fall down drunk!

I was nearly fourteen before I realized that this was not normal behavior. I had heard from one of her dearest and oldest friends that she had once been kind and loving, but that behavior was very alien to me. That person, I had *never* met.

Chapter 2

A Childhood Should Never Hurt

My family lived in poverty. There was no inside toilet or running water. I never knew if the poverty was due to the alcoholism or if the alcoholism was due to the poverty. It was my lifestyle, and it was all I knew.

My parents did not attend any of my school functions. Not one, including First Communion, Confirmation or even my high school graduation. There were only a handful of photos to mark my childhood milestones. It would be difficult for an outsider to recognize that a childhood had actually taken place. Adding to the sadness, I never had a birthday party, and Christmases were very meager.

Both of my parents were physically and verbally abusive. These were the days when hitting children was an accepted form of parenting. They didn't spank, they *hit*. Sometimes they would hit with an open hand, but most of the time it was with such force that it would send me reeling to the floor. I can remember as far back as age four being hit like that.

I also attended schools which allowed the hitting of children. Priests and nuns used hands, belts and rulers. I grew up thinking that those in positions of authority were no more than bullies. I had been taught that children had no rights and were of very little worth. Words that devalue, demoralize and/or demean can last a lifetime. What is said to a child matters! Hurtful, ill-spoken words can set a child apart from family, and also from future relationships. Feelings of inadequacy are deeply imbedded, and often rear their ugly heads throughout childhood, and adulthood.

The worst came when I was 16. I was brutally raped by a man eleven years my senior. I was found some 12 hours later and taken to the hospital. My mother never came to the emergency room, however she did phone in a request…"Make sure she's not pregnant!" I had never been with a boy and I had never had an internal examination. I was so scared, frightened and in such pain. If ever a girl needed her mother, this would have been the time. *She never came.*

My parents would not allow me to fill out a police report. My father did not want it *known all over town.*

The man who raped me went on to assault two other young girls within a year's time. He was eventually charged and prosecuted with those assaults. Just knowing that such brutality could have been prevented if I had been allowed to come forward was heart-breaking. If only!

Chapter 3

"Uppity Women"

My parents paid very little for my education. In fact, they invested nothing after my sophomore year in high school. My father referred to women who were educated past high school as "uppity women." I came to truly detest that phrase.

Left to my own choices, I chose to continue my education on my own. I began working at age 16 with any part-time job I could find after school and worked full-time every summer. I put myself through high school, college and later in life, through post-graduate studies. I somehow knew from very early on that an education was my only ticket out of the poverty and the pain of an abusive past.

Despite my dire home life, I carried a 3.86 GPA from my freshman year in high school until I finished my post-graduate studies. I was driven, and I knew that the responsibility for me rested squarely on my own shoulders. I could not hold anyone else accountable or expect anyone to carry me through.

By age 18, I had my own apartment, a full-time job and had begun college. I was on a mission! I *would* free myself from the memories of my youth. No one could hurt me again or reduce me to the point of the child unwanted. I was in control and could now work towards a positive, productive future.

Chapter 4

"Mr. Right"

By age 20, I had met my *knight in shining armor*, got married and moved 3000 miles from my childhood home. A brand new life was about to begin.

The very first time I met my new in-laws, they "blessed" themselves with beer cans! They were making a mockery of the only religion I had ever known. At that time in my life, this was the religion I knew and the only religion I devoutly followed.

For Catholics, the blessing of oneself is the outward expression of faith. At this stage in my life, I remained faithful to the only "religion" I had known since childhood. My faith was very dear and important to me.

I was left speechless and immediately mortified

by their actions. I had been *violated*. I had never been the victim of such bigotry, and I had no idea how to respond. I relied on my new husband to speak up for me. He said nothing...but he laughed *with* them! How could this be happening? I had always thought that a spouse was your protector... the one person who would always have your back.

Maybe my idea of marriage was just *wishful thinking*. Perhaps what I had always wished for, and dreamed about, truly did not exist after all. Maybe the future I imagined was unattainable in the real world.

Eighty-nine days after we were married, my husband deployed to Viet-Nam for 9 months. He insisted that I remain with his parents during his deployment. It soon became crystal clear, very quickly, that what seemed so right would become so wrong.

My in-laws would start drinking at 8 AM, and it would continue until well after midnight, daily. My father-in-law frequently made sexual advances toward me. He actually pinned me against the wall on two separate occasions. I was terrified of him, yet I had to live in his house. Who could I tell? Where could I go? I did speak with a local priest, but he gave no advice and offered no help.

When my husband returned home, we talked about his dad's behavior. He actually laughed and said, "Well, the old-man always did have a wandering eye for the ladies." The subject was never brought up again. I guess I knew *my place* after that – silence! It's the way it was from that time forward. If you didn't speak about it, then it simply did not exist.

My husband would soon follow in his parents' footsteps. Alcohol, once again, would play a major role in my life.

Chapter 5

A One-Parent View

The birth of every child should be an occasion for great joy, celebration and expectation. The birth of our three sons was an answer to my prayers. I could not imagine a greater blessing.

Unfortunately, this was not how my husband viewed parenthood. He was overseas, on his second deployment, when our first was born. It wasn't the miles that separated us. It was a mindset.

I was forced to stay with his parents during the pregnancy and birth. I had objected, but the decision had been made by my mother-in-law. I had no say in the matter. She picked out the doctor and had me sign an agreement stating that if, for any reason, my health became an issue, the pregnancy would be terminated. This was totally against everything I believed. My husband knew how I felt about the issue, yet he stood by his mother's wishes. It was as if I did not exist, nor were my beliefs of any worth.

My husband was always aloof and distant. He was very removed from my points of view. It was the non-involvement and the disconnected attitude that made me feel so alone. Even though he was home for the second and third pregnancies and births, he chose to spend the time waiting in bars. He was never by my side. No one ever held my hand, no one ever gave me encouragement, and no one ever shared that wonderful moment when you first meet your child.

The boys were not allowed to have birthday parties if he was home. He did become a cub-scout leader and little league coach for our eldest son. He did so with great reluctance and only because he continually said that he was more qualified. He never offered his services for the two younger boys.

All the years we were married, we never went out to dinner or a movie. We would attend a military dinner or gathering if it served him well. If it boosted his career, we would attend. I never received a Christmas, Mother's Day or a birthday gift from him. The marriage had sunk lower and lower, with less and less respect or love being shown towards me.

The one thing I did manage to hold onto was my Catholic religion. I continued to attend mass every Sunday with my sons. Even with my weekly attendance, I still felt very alone and empty at times. I knew I was unloved, and at this point in the marriage, perhaps I was only there to help boost a career. My religious beliefs seemed to be all I could hold onto. Everything else seemed to be drifting away.

Chapter 6

Tobacco Road

On one Sunday morning, while I was driving home from church, I was stopped at a stop light. My eye caught a glimpse of people gathered around an old battered, white washed church, sitting on the edge of a tobacco field. You could see these old churches scattered throughout the south, but I really paid no attention until this one morning. The sight fascinated me.

What really caught my attention were the sounds coming from the people gathered around that old building. There was laughter and even singing of some old hymns. These were the "hymns" I had heard on the radio as a child, but only until my father caught me listening to them and made me turn them off. He called them *heathen songs*. I always thought that was strange since I couldn't understand the Latin hymns I had to memorize!

I remember driving away thinking this must be what *pure joy* looked like!

A few days later, while shopping, I recognized one of the parishioners and told her how uplifted I had felt simply by seeing this outpouring of praise and joy. She invited me to join her on the following Wednesday evening. Now, who goes to church in the middle of the week? Me! I *did* go. My heart nearly leapt out of my chest. What joy! The singing, the praise, and most of all, I felt as if GOD Himself was in the building.

I was so excited, and could barely wait to tell my husband. He was furious! I never attended again, but I also never forgot.

Chapter 7

All-American Family

During the course of our 18 years of marriage, what appeared to the outsider as a picture of "pure Americana," was far different behind closed doors. The Naval officer with his perfectly groomed, well-mannered wife and sons was what people saw. However, the *grooming* went far beyond the public's perception. My sons and I were told what to wear, who would be our friends and who to entertain.

My mother-in-law picked out my clothes, and it was she who decided how much I would require for my monthly household expenses. She did all this from 3000 miles away! Yes, *she* decided my monthly military allotment.

Throughout the marriage, alcohol usage became more pronounced. The military lifestyle in the

1970's and 1980's was very conducive to the use of alcohol. People will always gravitate to those with whom they share a common bond. Every military event was preceded with alcohol and usually ended with alcohol. "Hail" and "farewell" lunches and dinners always followed this format. There were many of these occasions, and they would start at 10:00 in the morning and often last until well after 10:00 at night. Many military friendships and career promotions would depend on attendance.

The alcoholic, that was now my husband, became a very abusive man. When our youngest child was 18 months old, my husband "sat" for his children for the very first time. The boys had never been left alone in his care. I attended a wives club meeting, leaving the four of them alone for a little over 2 hours.

When I returned, I found the 5 and 9 year olds sitting in the same places as when I left. I thought this odd considering their ages. The youngest was in his crib crying so hard that he was shaking. I immediately knew that something was very wrong. When I changed him, I could not place two fingers between forming welts and bruises over his buttocks and upper thighs.

What could have caused such a horrific outburst of anger? What could an 18-month-old possibly have done that would have deserved this cruelty? He had been beaten by his "daddy": the person who was *supposed to* be his protector. Why this beating, you ask? The baby had cried during a Monday Night Football game!

My husband frequently back-handed the boys when they were young. This was exactly what I had endured as a child, and that was not going to be tolerated. I never again left my sons in his presence and unattended. He did, however, frequently, channel his anger towards me.

Chapter 8

The Affairs

There were numerous affairs during the marriage, but the one that dishonored me the most was one which involved my husband and my "best friend." Another took place in a hotel, and he took pictures of his partially nude "friend." He left these pictures in a shirt pocket. I often wondered if they were meant to be found. I suspect that they were.

I pleaded with my husband to get counseling or at least try again to speak with a chaplain. His answer was always the same. The problem must be mine because he had no problems! Once he told me to keep quiet, because if his commanding officers found out, his career would be in jeopardy. The harm to his marriage was of no concern and did not matter.

Finally, after a long day of drinking, I told him

to leave. I have no idea how I found the courage to say those words. The look in his eyes was terrifying. He choked me until I lost consciousness. When I regained consciousness, I was lying on the den floor. I had no idea how long I had laid there. He had gone to bed, not knowing if I were alive or dead. My children were asleep in their rooms, and if they had awakened, they would have found me lying there, motionless. I was paralyzed with fear, and I knew I could not wait for his next abusive move.

I called the police...it was over!

Chapter 9

Words Spoken

One of the most difficult things to overcome, if you come from an abusive background, are the unkind, ugly spoken words; words like *unwanted*, *stupid*, *useless* and *unworthy*, just to mention a few.

Those words are used by others to define you. If you've bought into these words and you believe them, then you've given the person who spoke those words authority over you. You will always be the person *they* say you are. Unfortunately, we become the beneficiary of that "authority." You MARINATE IN THE MADNESS! The walls start to go up, and we become bogged down. We are weighed down and overwhelmed. We give credibility to them. We easily condemn ourselves. Well, after all, somehow we'll never *measure-up*! Spoken words can be crippling and suffocating.

Even after being abused, betrayed and horribly unhappy, I was so afraid to end the marriage. How could I ever stand on my own two feet? How would I be able to support myself and children? After all, I was *used goods,* and certainly no one else would ever see any differently! How would I move away from the places of pain, failure and trauma? My mind was spinning and I had no one to turn to. I knew I had to move forward to protect my sons and myself. I'd find a way for us. I had to!

Sometimes I could barely breathe. It would require baby-steps, so baby-steps I'd take. As babies, we fall and stumble, but we get back up. Even babies heal from bruises caused by falling and bumping into obstacles. So, I would have to put one foot in front of the other until I could stand on my own again.

Chapter 10

A Mother's Failure

The years following my divorce were very difficult for me as well as for my sons. Our world was spun upside down. I was barely able to keep food on the table. Child support payments would arrive on time, only days later they would be returned as "insufficient funds." The ripple effect of these bounced checks would send us spiraling deeper into debt. At the same time, my "ex" and his girlfriend lived very comfortably; an 8-room house, and a new convertible was parked in the driveway.

When I dropped the boys off for weekend visits, I was not prepared for how I'd be met. I could not have imagined the embarrassment I felt for them and for myself. I felt sick to my stomach sending them to a house where sex, drugs and alcohol use was the accepted behavior. The girlfriend would meet us (by us I mean a 7 and 11 year old) at the door, wearing only a string bikini. Her son's room had a full frontal, nude female poster hanging on the wall. I couldn't block the images from them. I couldn't protect my children.

I was humiliated and broken-hearted for myself and my boys. These were not the days when the courts would intervene and the military "protected" its own. An attorney told me during the divorce process that my husband could do pretty much what he wanted, but if I even dated during that period of separation, a judge could find me an *"unfit mother."* That's how it was in the South in the late 70's and early 80's. I found myself without recourse, and I realized how much I had failed my sons. I had failed at the most important job a person could be given.

It was during one of the coldest Februarys in memory that brought me to the darkest of times. I was unable to keep gas in the car, food on the table, or heat in our home. I would work some 20 hours a day trying to do just that! I made an agonizing decision. I allowed my younger sons to live with their dad. He had the means to keep them fed, clothed and warm. I did not. A part of me died with that decision, and I have never been able to forget the pain of their leaving. The people I loved the most, the ones I had vowed to protect were gone.

The oldest son remained with me as we struggled through that very cold winter. Our home now was a 20- year old trailer, with a large hole in the floor, and plastic covered parts of the door and windows. Our heating fuel was syphoned by thieves not once, but twice that year. The second time, the house was so cold that the toilet cracked. We slept fully dressed including gloves and hats. The mice had come in as they tried to escape the harsh cold. It was then that my son and I became homeless. He went to stay with a friend, and I lived in my car.

Chapter 11

Hello Love

Close to two weeks after moving into my car, I was offered a motel room by woman whose husband I had once cared for. One evening, she invited me to join her and a few of her friends for a "girl's night out." I hadn't been *out* for nearly 19 years! I was thrilled at the chance to be *me*. Would I even recognize me again? That carefree person had long been forgotten.

During the course of that evening, I found laughter, good conversation and the opportunity and freedom to make new friends. Such simple things, but long ago put aside.

Shortly after dinner, I was approached by a young girl and handed a note. It read, "You have a smile that lights up the room. Won't you join us for coffee?" I was about to dismiss it, being a little embarrassed, until I saw where it had come from. Who I saw, I will never forget. He stood nearly 6 feet tall, with piercing blue eyes, and a little gray at the temples. Surely one of the women had put him up to this...*right*?

In fact, they had not!

I did not join him and his family for coffee that evening. It was two evenings later, at his home, with his family, after dinner! He in fact prepared dinner.

He was a retired Marine Major; a widower with two children. He had a son in college and a 12 year old daughter (the note bearer). I found out he was a family man, a purple heart recipient, and a man of deep faith.

We spent endless hours and months talking and getting to know each other. Fully knowing someone is a very intimate experience. You have to be invested in the relationship. We were!

If two people take the time to truly get to know each other, then they know the other's heart, their flaws and shortcomings. He knew me in my humanness. In the midst of all my imperfection, he loved me. He did not want to control or change me. He valued me. We would come to love each other as we were.

He created an environment of love, peace and worth.

In the months to come, he helped my oldest son finish high school, he lifted me up, honored my younger sons, and gave our love a promise and dignity. He attended my work functions and introduced me to his friends as his "lady love." He became my hero and the love of my life.

On a Friday evening, in a crowded restaurant, he dropped to one knee and asked me to be his wife. I cried for 30 minutes, but finally said yes. We made plans to announce our engagement to family and friends at a planned BBQ on Sunday...just 2 days away. This was the most glorious and the sweetest evening of my life.

Chapter 12

Freefall

I awoke to a glorious morning in early August. I was filled with hope and a joy that I had never experienced. I thought that the birth of my children had been the most important days of my life, and that fact will always be true. This was very different – it's hard to explain. For anyone who has never been loved, it's a feeling beyond compare.

Waiting to tell the world about our plans was the hard part. I had promised to wait until family and friends could share our happiness, so wait is exactly what I'd do.

I worked my normal shift and got home close to 4pm. As I pulled into my driveway, an EMT and fellow co-worker was waiting for me. He took my hand and told me that my fiancé had been killed in an auto accident earlier that afternoon.

I have very little memories of the next few days. All the joy, expectations, and hope just drifted away. The realization that all was lost began to set in. I returned to work, but was unable to function very well. I lost my job, and the younger boys returned to their father. They were, at that time, preparing to be transferred nearly 900 mile away to a new duty station. Then my oldest son joined the Army.

I was alone, without family, without hope, and without a reason to continue. I had never known such darkness. Everything good in my life vanished. I was in a vacuum, and there was no air left. A deep depression took over.

I remember closing the windows, turning on the gas, and waiting...

Chapter 13

From the Ashes

Through the haze and the darkness I heard the phone ring! I have no memory of walking towards a phone. I have no answer for why I picked it up! What possessed me? Somehow I gathered my wits, got up, answered the phone, and through the "fog" I recognized the voice of my former college professor. She was now a hospital administrator, and was calling to offer me a job as her assistant. She said that she had been trying to reach me for months to ask if I was available, and if so, when could I start.

It was a position that would eventually lead to my *dream* job. Nearly three years after accepting the first job at the hospital, I qualified to apply for the position of Director of Nursing. I had finished some further studies in my field, so now was the time to move forward. I applied, interviewed, tested and waited. Two weeks later came positive news. The job was mine if I wanted it! I accepted the position I had worked so very hard to gain; a position at one of the leading medical centers on the East coast.

I would soon be introduced to (and care for) some of the most influential people in my life today. I, unwittingly, was being catapulted into the world of the living. But maybe most important, into the world of *why* I was living!

Chapter 14

Introducing the Saints

There are two things I know to be true. First, if you're in a hole, STOP DIGGING! Second, and more important, the first step in asking for help is humility. I was about to find out that people are placed in our paths for reasons not quickly realized by us. For some of us, being humble and getting out of the ditch is a very long and winding path. I was about to be brought to my knees!

While I worked at the medical center, God positioned me to meet and care for some of the most ill people I'd ever had the privilege of serving. I consider these patients the *blessed saints*, put in my life to instruct me. Most suffered from advanced stages of cancer. Some were there for end-stage treatment and pain control, some for removal of diseased body parts, and still others submitted themselves to experimental procedures.

No one could ever give more than they. These were not only the blessed saints, they were modern-day *giants*.

One middle-aged woman had advanced brain cancer. Her cancer was so advanced that her eyes were kept taped shut to avoid being physically expelled from her body. She will always hold a special place in my heart. She would greet me every morning and ask, "How are you this fine, sunny day?" She was totally blind and could not have known if it was sunny or not. It didn't matter – it was always sunny in her world, and she made my world so much brighter. Her joy took my breath away!

It was the early 1980's when I met many newly diagnosed Aids patients. Some were children, and nearly all of them had been rejected by society. Ignorance and prejudiced ideas would not allow these precious children to attend school or to simply play with other children. My heart broke for those who were now denied basic human dignity.

My life was profoundly and forever changed, and sent me on a 15-year journey that would end up taking me on the ride of my life.

Chapter 15

Journey Forward

At this point, I started reading everything I could lay my hands on. I have always believed that the difference between where you are and where you want to be...is wisdom! I read the Bible, or at least I attempted it. I had great problems with the Old Testament. I just could not get past all the suffering, the treatment of women, the murders, and the concubines. OH THOSE CONCUBINES! Sometimes, I am convinced the human brain is not only the largest and most complex, but in some cases, the most unused.

It took me a great deal of effort as I attempted to understand. Sometimes I would just lay the bible back down and walk away, but it always drew me back. I sought advice and answers from pastors and a few biblical scholars. I especially had a difficult time processing all the laws and *regulations*. I suppose the Old Testament can be compared to our modern day tax codes. Our tax codes now have over 4 million words, and not even the experts and legislators can explain them! There was a growing list of religious regulations, and I think even some of the experts in Moses' law had great difficulty attempting to understand.

My understanding is very simple...the Old Testament was the "old law," while the New Testament is the Old Testament come to pass. With that knowledge, I continued to read about religion and religious practices, rituals, and legalisms associated with these practices. I read and studied for years. However, nothing seemed to offer that *love of God* thing my heart longed for.

It's a wonderful thing to know that God knows the answers before we know the questions. I kept being drawn to the God of my youth, although I had no idea just who that was, or *if* He truly existed. If He did exist, did He really care? Was I worthy to even call on His name?

CHAPTER 16

ME ON ME

I never felt *worthy*. I thought of myself as the *throw-away* child, and as a failure at being a wife and mother. I thought of myself as an unlikely candidate to come before this God. How could this *all-knowing* God see me any differently than I saw myself? Actually, with that thought in mind, what did I have to lose? Maybe this God wouldn't be either hindered *or* impressed by my resume. Was there some sort of tally, or perhaps a scorecard He kept? I was in trouble if that was true!

I decided to use my unused muscle—my brain— and kept on reading and studying. I found out we don't come to the Heavenly Father because of what we do or don't do. We come because of what *He* did. With that in mind, and with all my weaknesses, my journey continued. Whenever doubt came in, it was quickly gone. I was constantly being drawn back into an overwhelming need to know this God.

Under our own self-discipline and self-control, do we fail? ABSOLUTELY we do. For some of us it becomes a lifestyle! Whenever I ran away from my problems...all I got was tired! Many times in our efforts we come up short. It was now becoming very clear to me, that my need to know Him was the most important driving force in my life.

In the meantime, my sons were now 3000 miles west of me. They were all in different stages of their lives. I had missed so much. We had always kept in close touch and travelled back and forth from one coast to the other, but now I needed to place myself physically into their lives. I needed them, and I had no reason to stay alone on the East Coast.

I packed my car, myself and my cocker spaniel, and west we came. I left the dream job I loved and followed another path. This was truly a *leap of faith*. I had no house, no job, but I felt that I was being drawn back to my family, and towards a *new beginning*. This time I clearly got the memo, and this time, I obeyed.

Chapter 17

The "Great Shepherd"

Sometimes, before we come to know Jesus Christ, we grope and search in the darkness for *godly* things; grasping at spiritual things we don't yet clearly understand. We also seek "earthly answers." We look to politicians, idols, the gurus who sit on mountain tops, and to those with great wealth to whom we have given our power. We often go around in circles. The Israelites circled a desert for forty years. The journey should have taken about two weeks!

If we earnestly seek Him, He will gently call us. How do I know? The answer is very clear and simple. The God who says He will...WILL! He will call in *His* time. All we need to do is answer. One very clear way to answer is very easy. A simple, "Here I am, LORD" will do.

Hebrews 11:6 says, *"And without faith it is impossible to please GOD, because anyone who comes to Him must believe He exists and He rewards those who earnestly seek Him."* He longs to have us call Him.

After nearly 15 years of earnestly searching, a co-worker asked me to join her and her family at their church. And guess what? He was there. I FOUND HIM! I found Jesus; the loving Jesus who gave His very life for me! I started my walk towards Him and never looked back. Isn't it wonderful to know that God will call us *out* of the places we have no business being in? I started to open my heart to my Father, and as I did, I was being lifted into the world of a redeemed daughter. I would continue on this journey in the light of hope, *not* in the darkness of my past.

Luke 19:10: *"He comes to seek and save what was lost."*

Do you know why the shepherd's staff has a crook at the top? It's used to lift or to pull the lost sheep out of dangerous places, such as pits.

Hebrews 13:20 refers to our Father as not only the *Good* Shepherd but the *Great* Shepherd.

John 10:11 says, *"I am the good shepherd. The good shepherd lays down his life for the sheep."*

In the story of the prodigal son—in my case the prodigal daughter—one thought rings loud and clear. When we are only a speck in the distance, our Father will see us. God waits patiently and at a distance, but is always ready with open arms to welcome us home.

CHAPTER 18

WHO DO YOU SAY YOU ARE?

How do we live right with GOD? First, we respect *His* rules. Don't misunderstand the simplicity here. I don't mean to imply that obedience is easy. It takes a conscious effort, and the choices we make are very difficult at times. The outcomes of all our well thought out efforts are worth the work. There are a great many choices in this life, so we all need to choose wisely.

Matthew 5:1-10 offers powerful words spoken by Jesus. These are called the "Beatitudes." I believe everyone should take the time to read them, then be still, be quiet and let them wash over us.

In human words, it simply says how the Almighty has blessed each of us. They give us a better understanding of who we are.

Here is what the Beatitudes said to me:

I'm blessed when I feel I've lost. That's the moment when I find myself.

I'm blessed when I hit rock bottom, because that's when I realize that there is less of me and more room for GOD.

I am blessed in my darkness. GOD then becomes my light.

If I'm persecuted in His name, then I'll be driven deeper into His kingdom, and the heavenly angels will give a shout of joy and applaud me. It is then that I am in heaven's wonderful company and Satan is running scared!

The devil knows where faith lives. Make him afraid to be in your presence! God created you with everything you need to be extraordinary. In Him, you are exceptional...AMEN INDEED!

Everyone fails at one time or another. Some of us have made failure an art form! With all the failures I've experienced, God still loves me. I was an unlikely candidate, but my God pulled me up and is using me to carry His message. WOW! So, it is through great failures that we come to great faith. What God doesn't change, He will use. Chaos, struggles and difficulties usually result in profound strength and purpose. When you've lost your way, try going to the one who is *the way*. Sometimes you have to give up everything you know to gain everything you need.

Remember, God doesn't make junk! Look for His gifts *in* you. Let's not be earthbound in our thinking. We are made to soar! God created victory in us even before we faced any struggles.

God truly blesses my socks off!!! *Bold faith* is a catalyst. It will take you to heights that may be unimaginable to you now, but known to Him since time began. One person I know puts it this way: we are capable of having a "healing service" all by ourselves!

I have been blessed by the best children any mom could ever wish for. I have so many wonderful friends. They surround me and are a constant reminder of the greatness of God's love. I see GOD's greatness in the faces of my beautiful, precious grandchildren. I have been given an opportunity to bring glory to the LORD. How blessed INDEED!

Chapter 19

Let's Talk About Love

There's an amazing little book titled *The Message*. It's written by Eugene H. Peterson and published by NavPress. It's the New Testament in contemporary language. In the introduction for 1 Corinthians, Eugene says this:

"When people become Christians, they don't at the same moment become nice. This always seems to come as somewhat of a surprise. Conversion to Christ and His ways doesn't automatically furnish a person with impeccable manners and suitable morals."

In his introduction to 1, 2, and 3 John, he has this to say: "The two most important things to get straight in life are love and God."

I thought you'd enjoy those two quotations.

Love takes work, but the benefits are innumerable!

The apostle Paul speaks of the most important gifts of love in 1 Corinthians 13:4-7. These words are, to me, some of the most beautiful and profound ever written. It is no wonder that they are frequently requested at marriage ceremonies.

"Love is patient, love is kind. It does not envy, it does not boast, it is not proud. It is not rude, it is not self-seeking, it is not easily angered, and it keeps no record of wrongs. Love does not delight in evil, but rejoices with the truth. It always protects, always trusts, always hopes, always perseveres. Love never fails."

These words are often spoken, but how often are they *lived*? How many marriages would avoid divorce courts if we truly paid attention to the meaning? How many unborn children would have lived with the promise of a tomorrow? How many would have been spared pain and suffering at the hands of an abusive spouse? For those who live in oppressed countries, what would it be like to live in a nation that embraced this belief, rather than be forced to endure a cruel dictator's rule? If we had accepted this gift, would our society have turned to immorality, injustice, alcohol and drugs?

At times, we have failed ourselves and our children, and so have those who have harmed us in some way. All those things we have tried to fill the emptiness with, have ultimately failed. What we needed was always within our grasp, but we chose to ignore it.

We cannot forgive, forget, feel joy, or embrace people if we haven't learned the importance of love. Before we can love others, we need to find ourselves *worthy* of love. We cannot give to others what we don't possess.

1 Corinthians 13: 13 says, *"And now these three remain: faith, hope and love. But the greatest of these is LOVE."*

Love is my wish for you, and it is His promise.

CHAPTER 20

SAY A LITTLE PRAYER FOR YOU

Before I was born again (believed in and accepted Jesus as Lord), I never would have called myself a prayer warrior. I had grown up memorizing prayers, or asking a saint to pray in my name. I never realized that *I* could actually talk to God *myself*. Isn't that sad? All those years asking others to pray on my behalf, when all along, God was waiting for *me* to call His name with my own mouth! That's what prayer is...simply talking to God. No middle man is needed! I am only 5 feet tall, yet when I'm on my knees, I reach enormous heights. When I am alone with God, He always brings me to a special, honored place.

I believe that the shortest distance between a problem and a solution is equal to the same distance between your knee and the floor, even if you can only kneel in your heart.

Jesus didn't die for us so we could have another religion. He died so we could experience a close relationship with Him. Religion is man's way of coming to God. Christianity is God's way of coming to man.

Prayers heard in heaven (and they all are), make the angels sing with joy. Think of prayers as miracles. Therefore, there is a miracle in your mouth! When you talk with God, don't give Him an argument. You don't get to vote on the will of God. Don't start a dialogue with God by saying, "Listen Lord – for I speaketh." You are under *His* authority, not the other way around. There is no King Self! God listens to your prayers and He always, always answers. Sometimes, it may not be what we prayed for, but it will always be exactly what we need.

God is waiting on us to become verbal. Don't put Him in a box and only pull Him out when there's a crisis. We can find Him in the most unlikely places. Just call His name anywhere, anytime. Let's not wait until we're desperate. I started out saying *thank you* for all He had given to me.

I talk to God all day, every day. I thank Him, seek Him, and try to always listen to Him. One of my simplest prayers is..."HELP." I pray for my children, grandchildren, friends and even my enemies. I pray for love, forgiveness and peace. I pray for what I want, and then I ask that His will be done in case He has something better in mind. I pray for the removal of my earthly thinking. I pray for joy. My list can get very lengthy, but He'll decide what I need, so I'll just thank Him for His time!

I sometimes cry out and pray that my sons will come to know this wonderful Lord. I shed tears at times, and ask that this world come to its senses and honor the One who created us. If you don't know Him, I pray you soon will. Your life will never be the same. If you have come to know Him, you are blessed and it's your turn to be a blessing to others. Pass it on!

This is how Jesus taught us to pray. Instead of memorized, repetitive words, Jesus gave us *His* prayer. JESUS gave His disciples an example to follow:

Matthew 6:6-13: *"But when you pray, go into your room and shut the door and pray to your Father who is in secret. And your Father who sees in secret will reward you. And when you pray, do not heap up empty phrases as the Gentiles do, for they think that they will be heard for their many words. Do not be like them, for your Father knows what you need before you ask Him. Pray like this:*

"Our Father in heaven, blessed is Your name. Your kingdom come, Your will be done, on earth as it is in heaven. Give us this day our daily bread, and forgive us our sins, as we also have forgiven those who sin against us. And lead us not into temptation, but deliver us from evil."

This prayer treats God with the highest of honor. The prayer calls for Christians to pray and work for the ongoing advancement of God's kingdom, and that remains true to this day. Please let these most beautiful words wash over you.

Remember to give thanks. There are many, many gifts bestowed on all of us daily. And, we have done nothing to earn those blessings. Everything is given by God.

I have no idea where I heard or read this little story, but I think it speaks volumes. There was a 6th century politician who was imprisoned in Italy for treason. As he was awaiting his execution, he reflected on his lot in life and wrote, "Nothing is miserable but what is thought so, and contrariwise every estate is happy if he that bears it be content."

So, contentment is a personal choice. God can give you contentment. Once again, give thanks in *all* things!

Chapter 21

Faith vs. Fear

I believe that atheists are people who lack experiences of a loving God, and that perhaps they are afraid of what they don't understand and cannot see. When we are alone, without resources and stripped naked, that is when we resort to prayer. It is then that most of us cry out. I certainly cannot return to my yesterdays, but I can act in faith to influence my tomorrows. Don't be held bankrupt by past failures or pain. Place your yesterdays at the foot of the cross and stand firm in His peace today.

Webster's Dictionary describes fear this way:
Fear (noun): unpleasant emotion caused by expectation or awareness of danger
Fear (verb): to be afraid of

<u>If you're engulfed by fear:</u>
- You're swallowed up
- Devoid of optimism
- Stripped of joy
- Stagnant, gripped and held motionless, weighed down
- A builder of barriers, walls and strongholds

<u>If you are a person of faith:</u>
- You're set free
- You are filled with joy, a source of happiness
- You're not bound by a pessimistic attitude
- You're open, and boundless
- You see others and yourself in a more loving manner

As a former critical care nurse, I have witnessed that ominous, terrified look of fear on the faces of those who were unbelievers facing certain death. They cursed a "god," any "god." My heart broke for them, but they would find no comfort. There was nothing to say to ease that terror. On the other spectrum were those who found a peace so profound that they're demeanor would hold me spellbound. So many actually *welcomed* an earthly end as they passed on to God's open arms and His promised glory. The look of victory is truly miraculous.

The unknown of coming to Christ may be a little scary, but remember that we have an enemy that tries to put fear in us. He knows where faith lives, but he also knows where fear lives. Don't let fear reign. Sometimes we are fearful of what may be asked of us! Will we be persecuted or belittled?

Worse yet, will we be asked to speak up against injustice? Most likely! God will place us wherever He needs us, doing whatever He knows we can handle. It may be outside of our comfort zone, but it won't be outside of our ability. GOD equips us.

Satan has a way of stopping us dead in our tracks. That's his M.O. I believe there is a place for fear, but I want my trust and love for Christ to trump my fear. Fear just isn't in my vocabulary as long as I have Christ with me and He is *for* me.

Chapter 22

Tell Me Why Again

He picked me for such a time as this. Make no mistake, He came down to my world when He seemed so out of reach. No longer will I be defined by anyone else. My identity is known in heaven. God knew me before I took my first breath. God will always turn disappointment, heartbreak, and yes, even betrayal and loss for our good if we call on Him. It may not be all that we wanted, prayed for or planned. Our wishes may not always come to pass, and many unmet desires may stir up sadness and doubt. Unfulfilled desires don't have to take the joy out of life. God is the designer, so things are not left to chance. Open yourself to God's heart and He will become your joy.

Yes, God had a plan for me in this time and in this place. He did not seek or feel the need to check-in with me first. My approval was not necessary. That was a bitter pill for me to swallow at the time. I thought after all the heartache and betrayal, that the person in charge was me! Sometimes the questions are very complicated, but the answers are always His. Oh, there are still times when I want to do it *my way*. I like to call it my *scenic approach*! That never ends well. So, I surrender whatever "it" is, knowing He'll see me through it.

We humans are just that, *human*. We are stubborn, mistaken, and easily blindsided. Maybe these are the reasons we find ourselves knee deep in the muck and mire!

The Bible is filled with God's patience with His people. Take Abraham, David and Peter for example. We are in good company with those who travelled the roads before us. They also knew doubt and fear. They fumbled around, got lost, and denied even when the facts were right in front of them. Try not to ask *why...why did this...why did they...why not...why weren't You...*but keep in mind that God's sovereign workings are just that...SOVEREIGN! His viewpoints come from a much bigger understanding. He sees the end from the beginning.

His love is greater than any earthly man can ever comprehend.

Chapter 23

Pardon Me

Forgive: to pardon or excuse; no longer to blame or be angry with someone who has done you wrong.

Matthew 18:21-22: *"Then Peter came and said to Him, 'LORD, how often will my brother sin against me, and I forgive him? As many as seven times?' JESUS said to him, 'I do not say to you seven times but seventy-seven times.'"*

Within Judaism, three times was sufficient to show a forgiving heart. Peter believed he had been pardoning generously. But, true disciples of Jesus are to forgive without count. Forgiveness is Christianity in action. We must surrender our fears, failures and pain, or otherwise we will never be free. You can't know freedom without true forgiveness.

I surrendered myself to God on February 20, 1999, at age 55! You see, I didn't need an explanation any longer; no more rules or opinions. What I desperately needed was a revelation. God invites each of us to know Him with a sense of intimacy, *not* by intellect. We need to know Him with a humble spirit and a forgiving heart.

Over the years, I have been able to forgive those I needed to forgive, otherwise those acts of betrayal and brutality would have always held me in captivity. The most important gift anyone can ever give or receive is forgiveness. If I had chosen to hold onto the pain and sorrow, I would have been an active participant in the very sins committed against me.

By His shed blood and death on the cross, Christ forgave *all* sin. Who would I be if I held anyone unforgiven?

Forgiveness doesn't have an expiration date. We can't say we forgive someone and then dredge it back up tomorrow. LET GO! Do not keep a record of wrongs with dates, circumstances, and times about others. We need to remind ourselves every now and then that we forgave. We cannot be happy if we harbor any resentment. Resentment can absolutely slam the door shut on joy and keep it closed.

In Isaiah 43:18-19, God says, *"Forget the former things, do not dwell on the past. See I am doing a new thing."*

The next scripture verses are some of the most breathtakingly beautiful I have ever read, and I hold them in a special place in my heart. I pray you feel the same way. May they speak to your heart.

Colossians 3:13: *"...bearing with one another and, if one has a complaint against another, forgiving each other, as the LORD has forgiven you, so **you must forgive**."*

Matthew 5:44: *"But I say to you, love your enemies and pray for those who persecute you."*

In other words, when wronged and betrayed, Christians are called to forgive others. Forgiveness is something I work on daily. Whether it is the act of forgiving someone else or myself, it takes a conscious effort.

I want to leave this chapter on forgiveness with these passages from the book of Luke:

Chapter 23 states, as Jesus hung dying on a cross, He forgave His executioners. In verse 34, He asked His Almighty Father, *"Father, forgive them, for they know not what they do."* The next person Jesus redeemed and forgave as He hung dying was one of the criminals (robbers) hanging next to Him, as stated in chapter 23 verse 42. *"And he* [the robber] *said, 'JESUS, remember me when you come into your kingdom.' And Jesus answered, 'Truly I say to you, today you will be with me in paradise.'"*

Chapter 24

The Evolution of Me

"When you pass through the waters, I will be with you, and when you pass through the rivers, they will not sweep over you. When you walk through the fire, you will not be burned; the flames will not set you ablaze. ***For I am the LORD your God, the Holy One of Israel, your Savior.****"*
—Isaiah 43:2-3

I am writing this little book in hopes that if you're in a place of fear or pain, you just might come to the realization that *you are* a child of God. He knows you and all you are enduring. If you will just ask, He'll rescue you. He'll lift you up to His level. He's your Father! It's what dad's do. They protect, teach, train, and do so with a loving heart. How many fathers do you know who died for their child? I know of only one.

The night I was born, Jesus stood near, and maybe, just maybe, He whispered... "This child is meant to be!" I believe He says that about every one of His children. He knows our uniqueness, our capabilities, and our shortcomings. He loves us all as we are. After all, He is our creator and He doesn't make mistakes.

Here's how He has seen me through all of life's challenges:

My survival at birth...The Hand of GOD touched me.
My survival after a brutal rape...The Hand of GOD saved me.
An education against all odds...The Hand of GOD led me.
The birth of three beautiful sons...The Hand of GOD blessed me.
My survival from an attempted murder...The Hand of GOD protected me.
A loving man's presence in my life...The Hand of GOD caressed me.
The phone ringing in a gas-filled room...The Hand of GOD raised me.
The many, very ill patients who knew no bounds... The Hand of GOD taught me.

If you had asked me who I was many years ago, I would not have known. However, if you ask me today, I will quickly tell you, *I am His*! It's all so simple now.

I was asked a few months ago, if I could think of a song that would describe my life, what would it be? Without hesitation I answered, *Amazing Grace*!

It is through our brokenness that we realize our blessedness. I have been set free and no longer am I the child unwanted, the girl assaulted, the wife betrayed and battered. *I am* the blessed daughter of the Most High God. I am renewed, reborn and redeemed.

In Mark 5:19, Jesus said, *"Go home to your friends and tell them what wonderful things the LORD has done."* So, here I am, telling you what I have seen and learned. May you be lifted and forever blessed by my story.

Chapter 25

Life's Desserts

May you know hope so strong that all your fears crumble. May joy and complete peace come over you, and all those who are dear to you. May you experience an unimaginable, deep love. You *will* have all of these. They are His gifts to you.

Let me share with you one of my favorite poems, found in a Christmas card from years past (author unknown):

You have a ticket no thief can take
An eternal home no divorce can break
Every sin of your life has been cast to the sea
Every mistake you've made is nailed to the tree
You're blood-bought and heaven-made
A child of GOD, forever saved
So be grateful, joyful, for isn't it true?

What you don't have is much less than what you do

Many will tell you that there are no modern-day miracles. Not true! Open your heart and your eyes and see what is before you. Then, you may get a glimpse of what is to come.

How many times have you attended a luncheon or dinner and been told to keep your fork because dessert was coming? Well, HOLD ON TO YOUR FORKS, something so sweet and of miraculous substance is on its way!

*"Those whom I love, I reprove and discipline, so be zealous and repent. Behold, I stand at the door and knock. If anyone hears My voice and **opens the door**, I will come in to him and eat with him, and he with Me."* –Revelation 3:19-20

Please open the door and welcome Him into your life.

<u>A prayer for you:</u>

Dear God, for so long I've gone through life by myself. I've done everything *my way*. I either put You aside or totally cast You out. For all those lost moments, I am truly sorry. I realize now that You were there all along.

I'm asking You for forgiveness. I'm asking You to come into my life, Jesus. I'm surrendering to Your will.

Come into my life. Make me the person You intended me to be. I accept You as my LORD and Savior. Amen.

Questions and Suggestions

Chapters 1 and 2: Yesterday's Child and A Childhood Should Never Hurt

Question: Did you or someone you know have a difficult, painful childhood?

Suggestion: If you are a minister, a pediatrician, a teacher, or anyone who may be involved with children, please be very observant. Get involved, call the authorities, and report what you see or what you suspect. You are the only voice a child may have.

Chapter 3: Uppity Women

Question: Did you need to battle through strongholds and barriers to acquire an education?

Suggestion: Do you feel that the end results were worth the struggles? Know that if the outcomes are valuable and honorable, they are truly worth the effort. And, you are worth it.

Chapter 4: Mr. Right

Question: Have you "settled" for the wrong person?

Suggestion: Wait on the Lord! Let God's promise for you come into your life. Don't feel as if you have to settle for less than God has planned for you.

Don't try to do it alone. Don't go searching in all the wrong places. That will only get you all the wrong answers. God always has a better plan! ALWAYS!

Chapter 5: A One-Parent View

Question: How do you view yourself as a parent?

Suggestion: Take a deep breath and search your mind and heart before you rush to an answer. Your self-view may not be as worthy as you truly are. Or, you may be lacking in skills as a parent. Be honest. Talk with your children. See yourself through their eyes. If you believe you need help, by all means seek it.

Talk to your clergy, a counselor, and if necessary, always remove yourself and your child from harm. There are shelters available through the Salvation Army, Union Gospel Mission, and many churches offer women's shelters, or they can put you in touch with those who can help. Most of these organizations can also help with educational needs along with food and clothing. You are never alone. Many churches have food banks and can put you in touch with safe places. You are a child of the Most High God. He will walk with you and guide you. Simply call His name.

Chapter 6: Tobacco Road

Question: Did you have an ah-ha moment?

Suggestion: Think back to a time when a miracle was taking place right before your eyes. I bet you have experienced that moment, but maybe you didn't recognize it.

Chapters 7, 8 and 9: All American Family, The Affairs, and Words Spoken

Question: Does the outside world see what's inside your world?

Suggestion: It matters what goes on in your world. If brutality and betrayal occupy most of your life, please speak with someone you can trust. Don't try to "fix" the abuser by yourself. Don't believe that an abusive person won't harm you again just because they say they are sorry. Not only will the abuse continue, it will increase and become more aggressive. Please remember that intoxication is never an invitation or an excuse! And always ask for the Lord's help. He will never forsake you.

Chapter 10: A Mother's Failure

Question: If you're a parent, is there room for improvement?

Suggestion: There is always room for improvement no matter who you are or what you do. There was only one perfect person, and He died on a cross! We are mortal, imperfect humans. If you are a parent, then you have the most important, 24/7 job in all the world. So, who do you go to if you feel overwhelmed? There are counselors, physicians, and many other very learned people to choose from.

Along with earthly sources, remember the greatest Father of all...your Holy Father. He can come into your failures and shortcoming with the most perfect wisdom. Just open your heart.

Chapter 11: Hello Love

Question: Have you known that one, great, earthly love?

Suggestion: Do you remember how thrilled you were when the love of your life entered your life? Give thanks to the One who sent that person to you. What a blessing! Some people go through an entire lifetime without knowing that joy. How much greater is your Father's love for you. He sent His only son to redeem you. You will never know any other love so deep and enduring. Open your heart to His love, and you will then know a love like no other.

Chapters 12 and 13: Freefall and From the Ashes

Question: Have you ever reached that pivotal point of complete and utter despair? Were you lifted out of the darkness?

Suggestion: Please seek help before depression takes you to a place so dark and dank that you feel totally helpless. You are worthy of great peace and joy. Seek the Father's hand. He will lead you out of the darkness. Satan is the angel of darkness. Don't give him any authority over your life. Whatever has brought you to a place of despair can be eliminated by the healing hand of God. Use all the tools He may give you. He is the Great Physician, able to heal body, soul and spirit.

Chapter 14: Introducing the Saints

Question: Has anyone come into your life who forever changed your point of view?

Suggestion: God places people into our journey for reasons that, at first, are not understood. He always has a plan. You may not understand it until years later, but given time, the reasons may become crystal clear.

I do suggest reading the Reverend Billy Graham's book called "Angels."[1] It's well worth the time and so beautiful. In it he writes, "I believe in angels because the Bible says there are angels; and I believe the Bible to be the true Word of God."

---

[1] *Angels: God's Secret Agents, Copyright 1975, 1986, 1994 by Billy Graham, Library of Congress ISBN 0-8499-1167-2, Word Publishing*

Chapter 15: Journey Forward

Question: Has your journey seemed too bumpy and not worth the traveling time?

Suggestion: God's roadmap is the best GPS one could ever have. Seek Him always, and you will never travel alone.

Chapter 16: Me on Me

Question: As in chapter nine, how do you view yourself?

Suggestion: Write your story. How do you look on paper? What do you want others to remember about you? What do you want changed and why? What makes you tick? See yourself as others see you, then see yourself as your Holy Father sees you. You are a person of great worth. You are His treasure. He has set you apart from all others. You are a blessed child.

Chapter 17: The Great Shepherd

Question: Do you envision yourself as a member of His flock?

Suggestion: Listen for His call and come toward His voice. He will call, and at first you may not recognize it. Listen in quiet expectation. His arms await you.

Chapter 18: Who do you say you are?

Question: Do you see yourself as a chosen child?

Suggestion: You are an heir to His kingdom. It is your birthright to call yourself a child of God. He is your Almighty Father. Come boldly to His waiting arms.

Chapter 19: Let's Talk About Love

Question: Do you know how it feels to be truly loved? Do you allow yourself to feel loved? Do you allow others to love you?

Suggestion: You are greatly loved. God delights in you! Please allow His love to transcend all your shallow, earthly thinking that you may have, or about how love should feel and look. Until you know His love, you haven't known love in its deepest form.

Chapter 20: I'll Say a Little Prayer for You

Question: Do you believe in the power of prayer? Do you have difficulty finding the "correct" prayer words?

Suggestion: There are no "correct" prayer words. Prayers are words spoken to God. It's about you and Him. No go-betweens are needed. The Holy Spirit will guide your thoughts. Simply speak from your heart.

Chapter 21: Faith vs. Fear

Question: Does fear of the unknown keep you from moving forward?

Suggestion: Faith is a belief in the unseen. You cannot be worried or fearful and be in faith at the same time. Don't give yourself over to fear. You are worth so much more than that. Fear is a place where Satan lives.

Chapter 22: Tell Me Again

Question: Have you been blindsided, mistaken or unaccepting?

Suggestion: If you have been, you're in great company. We all misjudge and make incorrect assumptions. Pray for a more loving acceptance of those who may have wronged you. It's all in His hands, and His plans are so much greater than ours.

Chapter 23: Pardon Me

Question: Are you a forgiving person?

Suggestion: It was through God's loving mercy that I was able to forgive myself and all those who caused me harm or pain. I prayed for the ability to forgive. Forgiving takes a great deal of soul searching and prayer. If you ask for the ability to forgive, you will receive a "freeing" from whatever has held you in bondage. Lighten your load!

Chapter 24: The Evolution of Me

Question: Do you believe you are growing in faith or denying the power of faith? Do you know someone who, after accepting Christ, was a changed person?

Suggestion: If you step out in faith and accept Christ as your Lord and Savior, you will be forever changed. If you know someone who is a true believer, observe their behavior. You will see a joyful person before you.

Chapter 25: Life's Desserts

Question: Could you possibly be a "modern-day miracle?"

Suggestion: Yes, you are! And, on that joyful note, may blessings and sweetness forever be yours. Hold on to your fork!

Epilogue

I have always thought of myself as an unlikely vessel to be used to bring hope and God's Word to anyone. Well, God's plans are so far out of my scope of understanding. With that said, I do know that my life's experiences may help to release someone from Satan's grip.

Hope will always allow you to breathe a little easier. It's the hope and love of God that can turn us around. Your parents gave you a name, God gave you definition.

Things usually get worse before they get better. Sometimes, if not always, something will happen in life that will knock you to your knees! Fortunately for us, God knows us profoundly, and He will show us our faults. When He does, He will also give us the strength and courage to overcome.

Ask God to change you, if change is what you need. He knows what matters and what needs to be addressed. Allow God to work His wonders. Truly knowing your Holy Father will equip you with all the ammunition you need. Be forever triumphant. Keep in mind that lust, unjust wars, illnesses, vice, selfishness, sorrows, and heartbreaks are not from a merciful God. These acts are always satanic.

I spoke of some of the saints in my life. I once read that the wonderful thing about the early saints in the Bible was that they were human. They lost their tempers, they were testy, egotistical, hardheaded, impatient, and at times they even scolded God. Sound familiar? The saints made many mistakes, and like each of us, they also had regrets. We all have faults and blemishes. The only perfect man died a horrible death on the cross for the rest of mankind. And, like the saints of old, we have been accepted and redeemed just as we are. He waits with open arms to embrace you.

Take comfort in this verse from the beautiful, old hymn called "Just as I Am."

> Just as I am...Thy blood was shed for me
> And that Thou biddest me
> Come to thee
> O lamb of GOD
> I come

Come to your Lord and Savior. He's waiting with arms stretched open.

About the Author

Bonnie "B. J." Bruce is a retired registered nurse and legal nurse consultant. She is a motivational speaker, and is the founder/owner of a ministry called Defined By No Other. However, if you ask her what her favorite titles are, she will quickly reply, "Mom and Nana."

B. J. has volunteered her time and energy at women's shelters, correctional centers, Union Gospel Mission, and for the Red Cross. She is passionate about being an advocate for the battered and abused.

In her spare time, you can find B. J. in front of an easel and canvas or in the kitchen cooking for family and friends.

Hold on to Your Forks is proudly published by:

Creative Force Press
Guiding Aspiring Authors to Release Their Dream

www.CreativeForcePress.com

Do You Have a Book in You?

www.ingramcontent.com/pod-product-compliance
Lightning Source LLC
Chambersburg PA
CBHW061502040426
42450CB00008B/1455